I0820284

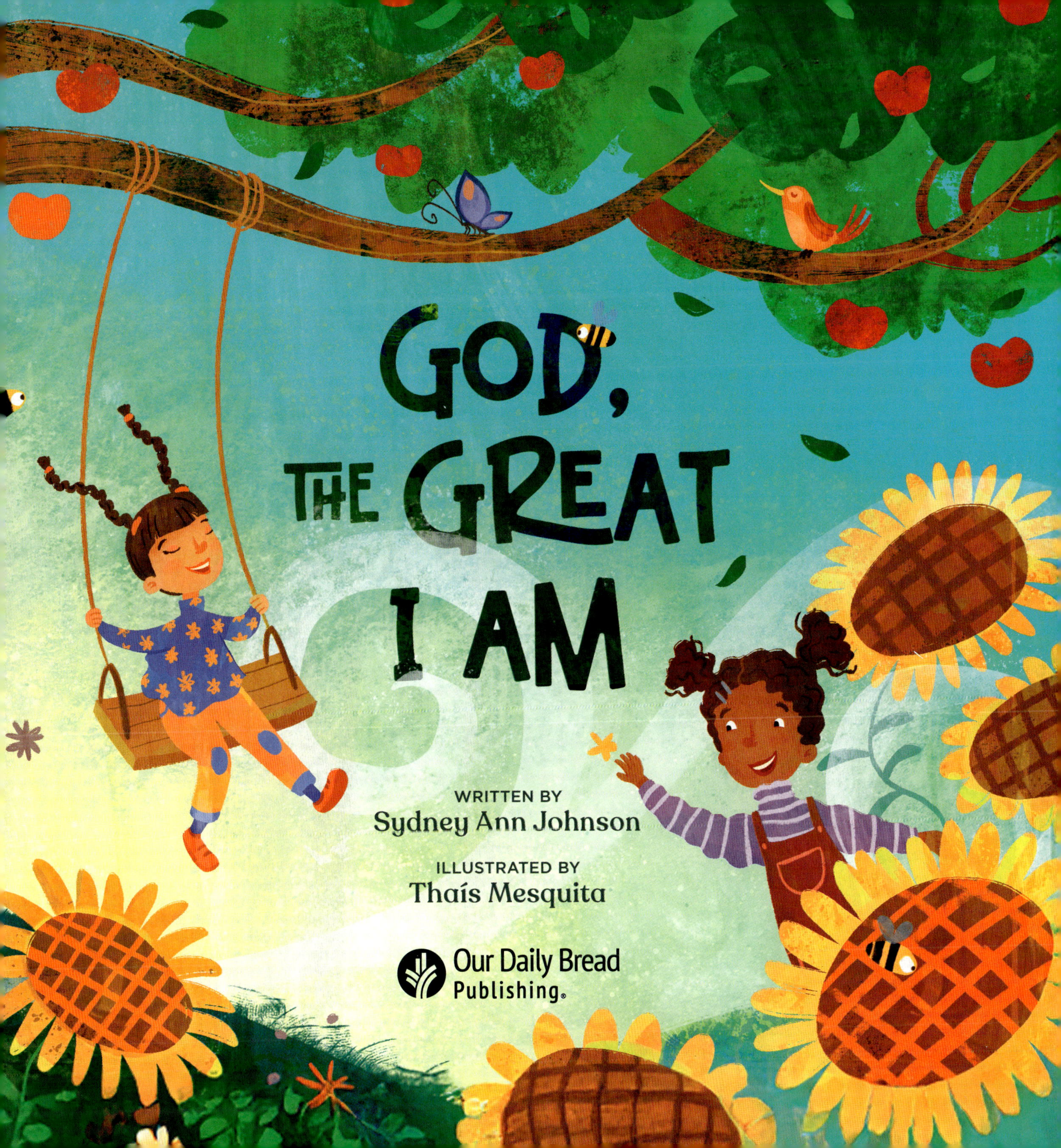

GOD, THE GREAT I AM

WRITTEN BY
Sydney Ann Johnson

ILLUSTRATED BY
Thaís Mesquita

Our Daily Bread Publishing.

God, the Great I AM

Author is represented by the literary agency of Embolden Media Group, Lake Mary, Florida, emboldenmediagroup.com.

ISBN: 978-1-64070-416-9

Library of Congress Cataloging-in-Publication Data Available

Printed in China
26 27 28 29 30 31 32 33 / 8 7 6 5 4 3 2 1

TO YAHWEH, who breathed life into my very frame,
whose love and kindness carried me on my journey
and kept me on my way.
My prayer is that Your children truly know they
are created in Your image,
fearfully and wonderfully made.
May you be glorified.

To my late mother **JUNE HAYES JOHNSON**;
I carry your love and freckles wherever I go.
I aspire to your boldness and unshakable joy.
Your resilience taught me I can always begin again.

With special thanks to **JEVON BOLDEN**,
who helped me keep hope alive,
because writing is a faith journey.

I AM...

I am the light that fills up the darkness
I brighten the morning with the burning sun
I settle the evening under the shimmering moon

Look above at the silver and gold stars
I scattered across the sky

I AM...

I am the one who spread the seas
far and wide and deep
I separated land from water
to give the islands their space

I push and pull the crashing waves
and only I can calm the ocean when it roars

I AM...

I am the first and the last, like the letters A and Z

I alone can create something

where there was nothing

I have no birthday because I always was and will always be

Though I never change, I keep the seasons shifting

I AM...

I am in the midst of the winter blizzard

where the wind howls and blows

I cover the evergreen forest with a brilliant, brittle frost
I taught the chipmunk to burrow, to keep warm in the bitter cold
until I wake the earth again

I AM...

I am the power that tugs the tulip
out of the earth after the spring rain
I awaken the cherry blossom to bloom
and give melodies to
the hummingbird to sing

I crack the cocoon of the caterpillar

to free the butterfly

I AM...

I am the one who sends the warm summer breeze
sweeping through the weeping willow's leaves
I make the firefly glow and give the bumblebee its sting

I set the eagle on the mountaintop
and place the rabbit in the field
providing each its home

I AM...
I am the giver of all good things
I bring the autumn harvest, full of apples,
pomegranates, and pears

I raise the tall sunflower
and turn leaves from green to
yellow, orange, and flaming red

I AM...

I am a promise-keeper through every season, every change

I invite my children to talk to me about anything

So bring me your tiniest little joy
and your biggest, deepest sadness

Ask me any question, tell me how you feel
and what you hope for

I AM...
I am everywhere at once—high and low
and in between
I watch you through the midnight hours
as you dream sweet dreams

There is never a place you can go without me
And I will never leave

I AM...

I am the divine designer
of the rainbow
and the waterfall

I decided strawberries would be red
and blueberries would be blue

And best of all . . .

I shaded people in magnificent varieties of brown, with melanin in every hue

I AM...

I am the one that put you snug
in your mother's belly
I set in place every freckle,
every dimple, every spot
I numbered all the hairs on your head
coily, curly, and straight—beautiful in every way

Before the beginning of time
I knew you

I AM...

I am the God of gods and Lord of lords
and my love will last forever

I created you for a reason
with a special purpose

To reflect my image—bright, creative, and compassionate
To care for my world—the big and the small
To bring honor to my holy name

I AM...
I am the God who can do anything
and all I do is good
I am the God who works mighty wonders
for all the world to see

I will be your helper and your friend
your God and your Savior

Place your hope in me
and I will show you

I AM WHO I AM

DEAR GROWN-UP:

Young readers need messages that empower them to embrace the distinct qualities hand-stitched into them by God, the Creator and Sustainer of all. As you move through your days, encourage them to see God at work, continuing to point out more evidence of God's greatness and presence. Every moment can be an opportunity for awe and an affirmation of God's love and intentionality. Consider keeping a record of your child's early observations and understanding about God. It will beautifully record his or her faith journey and help you set your own path to nurturing that faith. —Sydney Ann Johnson

The text for *God, the Great I AM* was inspired by the Bible's teachings. Consider reading or memorizing Scripture with your child to reinforce these eternal truths.

Genesis 1:1–31
Genesis 1:27
Genesis 8:22
Exodus 3:13–15
Exodus 14:21–31
Deuteronomy 6:4–11
Deuteronomy 10:17
1 Chronicles 16:34
Psalm 8:3–5

Psalm 24:1
Psalm 37:4–5
Psalm 40:5
Psalm 71:19
Psalm 104:14
Psalm 104:19
Psalm 139:13–17
Isaiah 40:28
Jeremiah 1:5

Daniel 2:19–22
Daniel 2:47
Luke 12:7
John 8:12
John 8:58
John 14:6
James 1:17
1 Peter 5:7
Revelation 1:8